HIS DAILY GRATITUDE JOURNAL

A BIBLE NOTEBOOK FOR MEN

WRITTEN & DESIGNED BY SHALANA FRISBY

COPYRIGHT 2018. ALL RIGHTS RESERVED.
WWW.123JOURNALIT.COM

Don't forget to grab your bonus freebies today!

WWW.123JOURNALIT.COM / FREEBIES

SCRIPTURE FLASHCARDS - BIBLE READING PROMPTS - JOURNALING PAGES

Copyright © 2018 by Shalana Frisby

All rights reserved. No part of this publication may be reproduced, distributed, or transmitted in any form or by any means, including photocopying, recording, or other electronic or mechanical methods, without the prior written permission of the publisher or author, except in the case of brief quotations embodied in critical reviews and certain other noncommercial uses permitted by copyright law.

More information at: www.123journalit.com

First Printing: May 2018
1 2 3 Journal It Publishing

ISBN-13: 978-1-947209-43-5
Pocketbook 6x9-in. Format Size
From the *Christian Workbooks* Series

THIS JOURNAL BELONGS TO

_ _ _ _ _ _ _ _

WHAT I AM THANKFUL FOR THE WEEK OF _____ TO _____

MONDAY:

TUESDAY:

WEDNESDAY:

THURSDAY:

FRIDAY:

SATURDAY:

SUNDAY:

MY NOTES & INSPIRATIONAL QUOTES:

WHAT I AM THANKFUL FOR THE WEEK OF _____ TO _____

MONDAY:

TUESDAY:

WEDNESDAY:

THURSDAY:

FRIDAY:

SATURDAY:

SUNDAY:

MY NOTES & INSPIRATIONAL QUOTES:

WHAT I AM THANKFUL FOR THE WEEK OF _____ TO _____

MONDAY:

TUESDAY:

WEDNESDAY:

THURSDAY:

FRIDAY:

SATURDAY:

SUNDAY:

MY NOTES & INSPIRATIONAL QUOTES:

WHAT I AM THANKFUL FOR THE WEEK OF _____ TO _____

MONDAY:

TUESDAY:

WEDNESDAY:

THURSDAY:

FRIDAY:

SATURDAY:

SUNDAY:

MY NOTES & INSPIRATIONAL QUOTES:

WHAT I AM THANKFUL FOR THE WEEK OF _____ TO _____

MONDAY:

TUESDAY:

WEDNESDAY:

THURSDAY:

FRIDAY:

SATURDAY:

SUNDAY:

MY NOTES & INSPIRATIONAL QUOTES:

WHAT I AM THANKFUL FOR THE WEEK OF _____ TO _____

MONDAY:

TUESDAY:

WEDNESDAY:

THURSDAY:

FRIDAY:

SATURDAY:

SUNDAY:

MY NOTES & INSPIRATIONAL QUOTES:

WHAT I AM THANKFUL FOR THE WEEK OF _____ TO _____

MONDAY:

TUESDAY:

WEDNESDAY:

THURSDAY:

FRIDAY:

SATURDAY:

SUNDAY:

MY NOTES & INSPIRATIONAL QUOTES:

WHAT I AM THANKFUL FOR THE WEEK OF _____ TO _____

MONDAY:

TUESDAY:

WEDNESDAY:

THURSDAY:

FRIDAY:

SATURDAY:

SUNDAY:

MY NOTES & INSPIRATIONAL QUOTES:

WHAT I AM THANKFUL FOR THE WEEK OF _____ TO _____

MONDAY:

TUESDAY:

WEDNESDAY:

THURSDAY:

FRIDAY:

SATURDAY:

SUNDAY:

MY NOTES & INSPIRATIONAL QUOTES:

WHAT I AM THANKFUL FOR THE WEEK OF _____ TO _____

MONDAY:

TUESDAY:

WEDNESDAY:

THURSDAY:

FRIDAY:

SATURDAY:

SUNDAY:

MY NOTES & INSPIRATIONAL QUOTES:

WHAT I AM THANKFUL FOR THE WEEK OF _____ TO _____

MONDAY:

TUESDAY:

WEDNESDAY:

THURSDAY:

FRIDAY:

SATURDAY:

SUNDAY:

MY NOTES & INSPIRATIONAL QUOTES:

WHAT I AM THANKFUL FOR THE WEEK OF _____ TO _____

MONDAY:

TUESDAY:

WEDNESDAY:

THURSDAY:

FRIDAY:

SATURDAY:

SUNDAY:

MY NOTES & INSPIRATIONAL QUOTES:

WHAT I AM THANKFUL FOR THE WEEK OF _____ TO _____

MONDAY:

TUESDAY:

WEDNESDAY:

THURSDAY:

FRIDAY:

SATURDAY:

SUNDAY:

MY NOTES & INSPIRATIONAL QUOTES:

WHAT I AM THANKFUL FOR THE WEEK OF _____ TO _____

MONDAY:

TUESDAY:

WEDNESDAY:

THURSDAY:

FRIDAY:

SATURDAY:

SUNDAY:

MY NOTES & INSPIRATIONAL QUOTES:

WHAT I AM THANKFUL FOR THE WEEK OF _____ TO _____

MONDAY:

TUESDAY:

WEDNESDAY:

THURSDAY:

FRIDAY:

SATURDAY:

SUNDAY:

MY NOTES & INSPIRATIONAL QUOTES:

WHAT I AM THANKFUL FOR THE WEEK OF _____ TO _____

MONDAY:

TUESDAY:

WEDNESDAY:

THURSDAY:

FRIDAY:

SATURDAY:

SUNDAY:

MY NOTES & INSPIRATIONAL QUOTES:

WHAT I AM THANKFUL FOR THE WEEK OF _____ TO _____

MONDAY:

TUESDAY:

WEDNESDAY:

THURSDAY:

FRIDAY:

SATURDAY:

SUNDAY:

MY NOTES & INSPIRATIONAL QUOTES:

WHAT I AM THANKFUL FOR THE WEEK OF _____ TO _____

MONDAY:

TUESDAY:

WEDNESDAY:

THURSDAY:

FRIDAY:

SATURDAY:

SUNDAY:

MY NOTES & INSPIRATIONAL QUOTES:

WHAT I AM THANKFUL FOR THE WEEK OF _____ TO _____

MONDAY:

TUESDAY:

WEDNESDAY:

THURSDAY:

FRIDAY:

SATURDAY:

SUNDAY:

MY NOTES & INSPIRATIONAL QUOTES:

WHAT I AM THANKFUL FOR THE WEEK OF _____ TO _____

MONDAY:

TUESDAY:

WEDNESDAY:

THURSDAY:

FRIDAY:

SATURDAY:

SUNDAY:

MY NOTES & INSPIRATIONAL QUOTES:

WHAT I AM THANKFUL FOR THE WEEK OF _____ TO _____

MONDAY:

TUESDAY:

WEDNESDAY:

THURSDAY:

FRIDAY:

SATURDAY:

SUNDAY:

MY NOTES & INSPIRATIONAL QUOTES:

WHAT I AM THANKFUL FOR THE WEEK OF _____ TO _____

MONDAY:

TUESDAY:

WEDNESDAY:

THURSDAY:

FRIDAY:

SATURDAY:

SUNDAY:

MY NOTES & INSPIRATIONAL QUOTES:

WHAT I AM THANKFUL FOR THE WEEK OF _____ TO _____

MONDAY:

TUESDAY:

WEDNESDAY:

THURSDAY:

FRIDAY:

SATURDAY:

SUNDAY:

MY NOTES & INSPIRATIONAL QUOTES:

WHAT I AM THANKFUL FOR THE WEEK OF _____ TO _____

MONDAY:

TUESDAY:

WEDNESDAY:

THURSDAY:

FRIDAY:

SATURDAY:

SUNDAY:

MY NOTES & INSPIRATIONAL QUOTES:

WHAT I AM THANKFUL FOR THE WEEK OF _____ TO _____

MONDAY:

TUESDAY:

WEDNESDAY:

THURSDAY:

FRIDAY:

SATURDAY:

SUNDAY:

MY NOTES & INSPIRATIONAL QUOTES:

WHAT I AM THANKFUL FOR THE WEEK OF _____ TO _____

MONDAY:

TUESDAY:

WEDNESDAY:

THURSDAY:

FRIDAY:

SATURDAY:

SUNDAY:

MY NOTES & INSPIRATIONAL QUOTES:

WHAT I AM THANKFUL FOR THE WEEK OF _____ TO _____

MONDAY:

TUESDAY:

WEDNESDAY:

THURSDAY:

FRIDAY:

SATURDAY:

SUNDAY:

MY NOTES & INSPIRATIONAL QUOTES:

WHAT I AM THANKFUL FOR THE WEEK OF _____ TO _____

MONDAY:

TUESDAY:

WEDNESDAY:

THURSDAY:

FRIDAY:

SATURDAY:

SUNDAY:

MY NOTES & INSPIRATIONAL QUOTES:

WHAT I AM THANKFUL FOR THE WEEK OF _____ TO _____

MONDAY:

TUESDAY:

WEDNESDAY:

THURSDAY:

FRIDAY:

SATURDAY:

SUNDAY:

MY NOTES & INSPIRATIONAL QUOTES:

WHAT I AM THANKFUL FOR THE WEEK OF _____ TO _____

MONDAY:

TUESDAY:

WEDNESDAY:

THURSDAY:

FRIDAY:

SATURDAY:

SUNDAY:

MY NOTES & INSPIRATIONAL QUOTES:

WHAT I AM THANKFUL FOR THE WEEK OF _____ TO _____

MONDAY:

TUESDAY:

WEDNESDAY:

THURSDAY:

FRIDAY:

SATURDAY:

SUNDAY:

MY NOTES & INSPIRATIONAL QUOTES:

WHAT I AM THANKFUL FOR THE WEEK OF _____ TO _____

MONDAY:

TUESDAY:

WEDNESDAY:

THURSDAY:

FRIDAY:

SATURDAY:

SUNDAY:

MY NOTES & INSPIRATIONAL QUOTES:

WHAT I AM THANKFUL FOR THE WEEK OF _____ TO _____

MONDAY:

TUESDAY:

WEDNESDAY:

THURSDAY:

FRIDAY:

SATURDAY:

SUNDAY:

MY NOTES & INSPIRATIONAL QUOTES:

WHAT I AM THANKFUL FOR THE WEEK OF _____ TO _____

MONDAY:

TUESDAY:

WEDNESDAY:

THURSDAY:

FRIDAY:

SATURDAY:

SUNDAY:

MY NOTES & INSPIRATIONAL QUOTES:

WHAT I AM THANKFUL FOR THE WEEK OF _____ TO _____

MONDAY:

TUESDAY:

WEDNESDAY:

THURSDAY:

FRIDAY:

SATURDAY:

SUNDAY:

MY NOTES & INSPIRATIONAL QUOTES:

WHAT I AM THANKFUL FOR THE WEEK OF _____ TO _____

MONDAY:

TUESDAY:

WEDNESDAY:

THURSDAY:

FRIDAY:

SATURDAY:

SUNDAY:

MY NOTES & INSPIRATIONAL QUOTES:

WHAT I AM THANKFUL FOR THE WEEK OF _____ TO _____

MONDAY:

TUESDAY:

WEDNESDAY:

THURSDAY:

FRIDAY:

SATURDAY:

SUNDAY:

MY NOTES & INSPIRATIONAL QUOTES:

WHAT I AM THANKFUL FOR THE WEEK OF _____ TO _____

MONDAY:

TUESDAY:

WEDNESDAY:

THURSDAY:

FRIDAY:

SATURDAY:

SUNDAY:

MY NOTES & INSPIRATIONAL QUOTES:

WHAT I AM THANKFUL FOR THE WEEK OF _____ TO _____

MONDAY:

TUESDAY:

WEDNESDAY:

THURSDAY:

FRIDAY:

SATURDAY:

SUNDAY:

MY NOTES & INSPIRATIONAL QUOTES:

WHAT I AM THANKFUL FOR THE WEEK OF _____ TO _____

MONDAY:

TUESDAY:

WEDNESDAY:

THURSDAY:

FRIDAY:

SATURDAY:

SUNDAY:

MY NOTES & INSPIRATIONAL QUOTES:

WHAT I AM THANKFUL FOR THE WEEK OF _____ TO _____

MONDAY:

TUESDAY:

WEDNESDAY:

THURSDAY:

FRIDAY:

SATURDAY:

SUNDAY:

MY NOTES & INSPIRATIONAL QUOTES:

WHAT I AM THANKFUL FOR THE WEEK OF _____ TO _____

MONDAY:

TUESDAY:

WEDNESDAY:

THURSDAY:

FRIDAY:

SATURDAY:

SUNDAY:

MY NOTES & INSPIRATIONAL QUOTES:

WHAT I AM THANKFUL FOR THE WEEK OF _____ TO _____

MONDAY:

TUESDAY:

WEDNESDAY:

THURSDAY:

FRIDAY:

SATURDAY:

SUNDAY:

MY NOTES & INSPIRATIONAL QUOTES:

WHAT I AM THANKFUL FOR THE WEEK OF _____ TO _____

MONDAY:

TUESDAY:

WEDNESDAY:

THURSDAY:

FRIDAY:

SATURDAY:

SUNDAY:

MY NOTES & INSPIRATIONAL QUOTES:

WHAT I AM THANKFUL FOR THE WEEK OF _____ TO _____

MONDAY:

TUESDAY:

WEDNESDAY:

THURSDAY:

FRIDAY:

SATURDAY:

SUNDAY:

MY NOTES & INSPIRATIONAL QUOTES:

WHAT I AM THANKFUL FOR THE WEEK OF _____ TO _____

MONDAY:

TUESDAY:

WEDNESDAY:

THURSDAY:

FRIDAY:

SATURDAY:

SUNDAY:

MY NOTES & INSPIRATIONAL QUOTES:

WHAT I AM THANKFUL FOR THE WEEK OF _____ TO _____

MONDAY:

TUESDAY:

WEDNESDAY:

THURSDAY:

FRIDAY:

SATURDAY:

SUNDAY:

MY NOTES & INSPIRATIONAL QUOTES:

WHAT I AM THANKFUL FOR THE WEEK OF _____ TO _____

MONDAY:

TUESDAY:

WEDNESDAY:

THURSDAY:

FRIDAY:

SATURDAY:

SUNDAY:

MY NOTES & INSPIRATIONAL QUOTES:

WHAT I AM THANKFUL FOR THE WEEK OF _____ TO _____

MONDAY:

TUESDAY:

WEDNESDAY:

THURSDAY:

FRIDAY:

SATURDAY:

SUNDAY:

MY NOTES & INSPIRATIONAL QUOTES:

WHAT I AM THANKFUL FOR THE WEEK OF _____ TO _____

MONDAY:

TUESDAY:

WEDNESDAY:

THURSDAY:

FRIDAY:

SATURDAY:

SUNDAY:

MY NOTES & INSPIRATIONAL QUOTES:

WHAT I AM THANKFUL FOR THE WEEK OF _____ TO _____

MONDAY:

TUESDAY:

WEDNESDAY:

THURSDAY:

FRIDAY:

SATURDAY:

SUNDAY:

MY NOTES & INSPIRATIONAL QUOTES:

WHAT I AM THANKFUL FOR THE WEEK OF _____ TO _____

MONDAY:

TUESDAY:

WEDNESDAY:

THURSDAY:

FRIDAY:

SATURDAY:

SUNDAY:

MY NOTES & INSPIRATIONAL QUOTES:

Printed in Great Britain
by Amazon